GUANAJUATO

Travel Guide 2024

Discover the Best of México's Historic Gem; Must-See Attractions, Local Secrets, and Travel Tips for a Memorable Vacation.

Wendy T. Sierra

Copyright

Table of Contents

Forward

Welcome to the vibrant and enchanting world of Guanajuato, Mexico. This travel guide is your key to unlocking the secrets of one of the most captivating cities I've ever had the pleasure to explore. My first visit to Guanajuato was an unexpected detour, but it quickly became a highlight of my travels. The city's narrow, winding alleys and colorful facades seemed like a scene straight out of a fairytale.

I still remember the warm welcome from the locals at Mercado Hidalgo, where a vendor insisted I try a slice of his fresh mango, seasoned with chili powder and lime. That small gesture of hospitality set the tone for the rest of my journey. Whether it was sharing laughs with fellow travelers during a lively callejoneada or marveling at the intricate architecture of Teatro Juárez, each moment in Guanajuato felt like a treasure waiting to be discovered.

This guide aims to provide you with not just the must-see attractions but also the hidden gems that make Guanajuato unique. From the serene Sierra de Santa Rosa to the bustling artisan markets, there's something here for every traveler. You'll find tips on sustainable travel, recommendations for family-friendly activities, and insights into the local culture and cuisine.

As you flip through these pages, I hope you'll feel the same sense of wonder and excitement that I did. Guanajuato is more than a destination; it's an experience that stays with you long after you've returned home. So pack your bags, open your heart, and get ready for an unforgettable adventure. **Welcome to Guanajuato!**

Introduction

Guanajuato, a Mexican city set between soaring mountains and brimming with colonial splendor, entices visitors seeking a compelling combination of history, culture, and lively energy. This chapter will serve as your introduction to this interesting location, providing an overview, a look into its historic past, and information on how to begin your Guanajuato trip.

Overview of Guanajuato

Guanajuato, the capital of the same-named state, is a city that proudly displays its heritage. Guanajuato, founded in the 16th century after the discovery of a silver vein, rapidly became an important mining hub in the Spanish viceroyalty of New Spain. This affluence fostered the development of large colonial structures, churches embellished with baroque details, and a network of underground tunnels that snake beneath the city. Guanajuato now flourishes as a cultural hotspot, with cobblestone streets filled with students from the famed University of Guanajuato, vibrant residents, and interested tourists.

Beyond its historical heart, Guanajuato has a vibrant artistic scene. Muralists have splattered their colorful works on walls, while street entertainers have added their melodies to the city's symphony. A famous culinary scene tantalizes taste buds with regional delicacies, while at night, the city turns into a dynamic glow of live music venues and buzzing clubs.

Guanajuato's modest size allows for easy exploration on foot, with secret plazas and quaint eateries nestled around every corner. For those looking for a thrill, a unique kind of public transportation, the funicular train, climbs a high slope and provides stunning panoramic vistas.

Historical & Cultural Significance

Guanajuato's storyline is inextricably linked to Mexico's. The discovery of silver in 1540 catapulted the city to the international spotlight. Spanish conquistadors swarmed the area, creating mines and altering the terrain. The wealth mined from these depths spurred the building of beautiful churches, like the famed La Basílica Colegiata de Nuestra Señora de Guanajuato, and opulent homes, demonstrating the city's richness.

However, Guanajuato's success had a human cost. Thousands of indigenous people were subjected to harsh working conditions in the mines, while African slaves were brought in to complement the workforce. This time left a lasting effect on the city's cultural fabric, as seen by rituals and songs that continue to resonate today.

The war for Mexican independence also took place on Guanajuato's stage. In 1810, Miguel Hidalgo y Costilla, a Catholic priest, issued the Grito de Dolores (Cry of Dolores), which sparked the Mexican War of Independence. The city's Alhóndiga de Granaditas, a former grain storage facility, became a battleground and is now a museum remembering the liberation struggle.

Guanajuato continued to evolve after it gained independence. The mining economy varied, but the city remade itself as a hub of education and culture. The University of Guanajuato, founded in 1822, nurtured a dynamic intellectual culture, drawing professors and artists who helped form the city's character.

Guanajuato's cultural significance goes beyond its historical sites. The annual Cervantino Worldwide Festival, held in the fall, is a well-known festival of arts and culture that draws worldwide artists, musicians, and theatrical companies. Throughout the year, colorful street entertainers, like the adorable callejoneadas (strolling musicians), serenade visitors with traditional melodies and fill the city with a positive vibe.

How to Get There

Guanajuato is surprisingly accessible, with numerous possibilities depending on your starting place. The closest major airport is in León, about 90 kilometers distant. From there, you may take frequent buses and shuttles to Guanajuato. Consider taking the train from Mexico City, which provides a pleasant and lovely tour through the Central Mexican countryside.

If you're already exploring other regions of Mexico, Guanajuato is centrally positioned and easy to incorporate into your vacation schedule. Many long-distance buses connect the city with renowned tourist locations such as San Miguel de Allende and Guadalajara.

Once you arrive, Guanajuato's modest size makes walking the most gratifying method to enjoy its beauty. Taxis are easily accessible for longer distances, and the unusual funicular train provides a fascinating and picturesque way to negotiate the city's high inclines.

So, pack your walking shoes and spirit of exploration, and be ready to be enchanted by Guanajuato's magic. This lovely city awaits, eager to share its rich history, lively culture, and irresistible beauty.

Plan Your Trip

With Guanajuato calling, it's time to turn that fantasy into reality! This chapter provides you with the necessary information to organize your ideal Guanajuato experience.

Best Time To Visit

Guanajuato has a good year-round climate, however, the "best" time to visit is dependent on your interests. Here's a breakdown to help you choose:

Spring (March-May): Guanajuato is painted in bright colors, with blooming jacaranda trees giving a touch of purple enchantment. The weather is pleasant, making it ideal for discovering the city's hidden gems. However, this is peak tourist season, so anticipate bigger people and somewhat higher rates.

Summer (June–August): The summer heat warms Guanajuato, making it ideal for visiting outdoor cafés and rooftop patios. However, afternoon rains are frequent, so bring an umbrella or a light raincoat. Hotel rates may also be at their peak during this time.

Fall (September-November): Fall is undoubtedly the best season to visit Guanajuato. The crowds thin out, the weather remains warm and bright, and the annual Cervantino International Festival bursts with a spectacular exhibition of arts and culture. Make sure to secure your lodgings well in advance for this popular event.

Winter (December-February): Winter has the coldest temperatures, making it excellent for individuals who wish to avoid the heat. Posada activities running up to Christmas fill the city with a festive vibe, and accommodation prices are often lower. However, certain attractions' hours may be curtailed during this period.

Insider Tip: I once went to Guanajuato for the Day of the Dead celebrations in early November. The city became a vivid display of colorful altars, exuberant parades, and a spirit of happy memory. It was a genuinely memorable experience.

Visa Requirements

The visa requirements for entering Mexico differ according to your nationality. Check with your local Mexican embassy or consulate well in advance of your travel to discover what documentation you will require. Citizens of the United States, Canada, and most European nations can usually receive a tourist visa upon arrival in Mexico, but they must have a valid passport and proof of onward travel.

Travel Essentials

Here's a checklist to ensure you're prepared for your Guanajuato adventure:

Comfortable Walking Shoes: Guanajuato is a walker's heaven, so bring footwear that can tolerate cobblestone streets and hilly terrain.

Sunscreen & Hat: The Mexican sun may be fierce, so wear sunscreen and a wide-brimmed hat, especially during the summer months.

Light Rain Jacket: As previously said, afternoon rains are possible, so bring a light rain jacket just in case.

Pesos: While some shops take US dollars, it's always a good idea to have Mexican pesos on hand for modest purchases and street sellers. ATMs are widely available in Guanajuato.

Spanish Phrasebook: While English is spoken in certain tourist destinations, learning a few basic Spanish phrases can help you interact with the locals and have a better experience.

Camera: Use a camera to capture Guanajuato's magical atmosphere. Do not forget to bring spare batteries and memory cards!

Sense of Adventure: Guanajuato is brimming with hidden treasures waiting to be uncovered. Embrace the unexpected and be ready to fall in love with the city's charm.

Pro Tip: I usually bring a reusable water bottle when I travel. It's not only environmentally beneficial, but it also saves you money on bottled water, which is especially useful on lengthy hikes across the city.

Local Transportation

Once you get to Guanajuato, navigating the city is simple. Here are the transit options:

Walking: As previously said, Guanajuato is best visited on foot. This allows you to absorb up the ambiance, find secret plazas, and come upon unexpected treasures.

Taxis: Taxis are easily accessible and a suitable choice for longer journeys or when your feet are tired. To avoid surprises, agree on the cuisine ahead of time.

Funicular Train: This one-of-a-kind public transit system features a funicular train that climbs a high slope to provide spectacular panoramic views of the city. It's a must-try for any tourist.

Buses: Local buses link Guanajuato to adjacent cities and villages, making it an ideal day trip destination.

Local Flavor: Consider hiring a bicycle taxi, or "bici taxi," for a one-of-a-kind and environmentally responsible way to get around town. These colorful pedal-powered taxis give a local flair to your trip and are a fun way to get around, especially on flat terrain.

This chapter will help you arrange a wonderful vacation to Guanajuato. Remember that the enchantment of this city is found not only in its historical sites, but also in its colorful streets, friendly locals, and unexpected interactions.

Where to Stay in Guanajuato

Choosing the proper place to stay may substantially improve your trip experience in Guanajuato. Guanajuato has a wide choice of lodgings to meet the interests and tastes of every tourist, from sumptuous luxury hotels to low-cost options and one-of-a-kind boutique stays. Here's a detailed guide to finding the ideal hotel for your vacation.

Luxury Hotels and Resorts

For those looking for the ultimate in comfort and facilities, Guanajuato boasts various luxury hotels and resorts that guarantee an amazing stay.

Villa María Cristina: This boutique hotel, a member of the Small Luxury Hotels of the World, combines elegance and comfort. It is located in a historic structure and offers magnificent accommodations, a world-class spa, and gourmet dining options. The wonderfully planted grounds and swimming pool offer a peaceful respite after a day of touring.

Hotel Boutique 1850: Located in the center of Guanajuato City, this luxury hotel blends historical elegance with modern comforts. Each room is beautifully furnished, and the rooftop patio provides breathtaking views of the city. The hotel's closeness to the main sites makes it an excellent choice for touring.

Rosewood San Miguel de Allende: While not located in Guanajuato City proper, this luxury resort in adjacent San Miguel de Allende is worth considering. It features large suites, a full-service spa, and a variety of dining options, all situated on beautifully groomed grounds. The resort's meticulous attention to detail and great service make it an excellent choice for a luxurious vacation.

Budget-Friendly Options

Travelers on a budget can discover a variety of economical lodgings in Guanajuato that provide comfort and convenience without breaking the bank.

Hostal Casa de Dante: This bustling hostel is ideal for budget-conscious travelers. It offers both individual and dormitory rooms, as well as a rooftop patio with panoramic views of the city. The courteous staff and shared kitchen foster a welcoming environment, making it simple to meet other visitors.

Hotel Real de Leyendas: Located within walking distance of several of Guanajuato's top attractions, this low-cost hotel provides clean, comfortable rooms at a fair rate. The hotel's colonial-style architecture and pleasant staff make it a popular choice for budget guests.

Casa Bertha: Casa Bertha, a family-run guesthouse, offers a welcoming atmosphere and reasonable pricing. The rooms are modest but pleasant, and the rooftop patio provides excellent views of the city. Its central location allows visitors to easily see Guanajuato's sites on foot.

Unique Accommodations & Boutique Hotels

For a more unique experience, try staying at one of Guanajuato's unique boutique hotels or other alternative lodging options.

El Mesón de los Poetas: This beautiful boutique hotel is styled after great poets, with each room honoring a different literary personality. The hotel's beautiful decor and historic architecture offer a welcoming and inspirational environment. Guests will appreciate the central courtyard and the hotel's excellent position in the center of the city.

Casa Zuniga B&B: Perched on a hillside with breathtaking views of Guanajuato, this bed and breakfast provides a one-of-a-kind experience with a personal touch. Rick, the proprietor, is recognized for his warmth and provides guided tours of the city. The rooms are distinctively furnished, and the prepared breakfast is a favorite among many guests.

La Casa de Frida: This vibrant boutique hotel honors the renowned Mexican artist Frida Kahlo. Each apartment has brilliant colors and artwork inspired by Kahlo's life and work. The hotel's cozy setting and artistic flare make it an unforgettable place to stay.

Tips for Selecting Good Accommodations

Choosing the appropriate accommodations may significantly improve your vacation to Guanajuato. Here are some guidelines to help you make the best decision:

Consider Location: If you intend to visit Guanajuato's historic core, consider hotels that are close to key attractions. Staying in the city center gives you easy access to attractions, restaurants, and stores without the need for transportation.

Determine Your Budget: Before you begin looking for hotels, you should establish your budget. Guanajuato has a variety of accommodations, from inexpensive hostels to luxury hotels. Knowing your budget will help you reduce your options and avoid overpaying.

Look for Facilities: Consider which facilities are essential to you. Whether it's free Wi-Fi, a swimming pool, or an on-site restaurant, making a list of must-have features can help you locate the ideal location to stay.

Read Reviews: Look for internet reviews from past visitors to get a sense of what to anticipate. Websites like TripAdvisor and Booking.com give useful information on the quality and service of various lodgings.

Book Early: Guanajuato is a popular tourist destination, especially during events such as the Cervantino. To reserve your favorite accommodation, book early in advance, especially during high travel seasons.

Finally, Guanajuato has a wide range of hotels to meet the demands of any guest. Whether you want elegance, affordability, or distinctive charm, you'll find the ideal spot to relax and recharge as you explore this interesting city. By evaluating your tastes and conducting some research, you may ensure a pleasant and memorable vacation in Guanajuato.

Must-See Attractions

Guanajuato's allure is evident not just in its cobblestone streets and bustling plazas, but also in its fascinating assortment of historical and cultural sites. This chapter provides a tour of some of the city's must-see attractions, ensuring you don't miss a beat.

Alhóndiga de Granaditas

The Alhóndiga de Granaditas' walls hint at Guanajuato's past. This enormous fortress-like structure, originally built in the 18th century as a

grain storage facility, was essential in Mexico's war for independence. In 1810, a Catholic priest named Miguel Hidalgo y Costilla led a group of revolutionaries in a daring raid on the Alhóndiga, initiating the Mexican War of Independence. Today, the structure has been turned into a museum, its hallways reverberating with stories of valor and sacrifice.

A Walk Through History: I distinctly recall examining the Alhóndiga's exhibitions, each carefully arranged to transport you back in time. One segment depicts the armament employed during the siege, while another describes the daily life of those who defended the structure. The highlight for me was being on the same rooftop where the insurgents started their attack, which provided a panoramic perspective of the city and sparked my imagination.

Beyond the Battles: The Alhóndiga de Granaditas provides more than simply a history lesson. The museum also holds a wonderful collection of pre-Columbian artifacts, which provide insight into the region's rich indigenous legacy before the advent of the Spanish.

Mummy Museum (Museo de Las Momias)

For those who enjoy the odd, the Guanajuato Mummy Museum provides a memorable experience. This museum, built in a former cemetery, shows naturally mummified remains that were accidentally excavated during the nineteenth century. The arid environment and unusual soil conditions resulted in a natural mummification process, preserving these remains in an odd yet wonderfully appealing manner.

A Glimpse into Mortality: While some may find the exhibit disturbing, I found it quite thought-provoking. Walking through the glass

exhibit cases, I was fascinated by the stories written on the faces of these mummified people. Each one demonstrates the fragility of existence and the everlasting power of time. The museum also dives into the scientific explanations behind the mummification process, which adds educational value to the trip.

Insider Tip: If you are easily startled, this museum may not be for you. If you're looking for a unique and thought-provoking experience, the Mummy Museum provides an intriguing view into Guanajuato's history and the secrets of human mortality.

Juárez Theater (Teatro Juárez)

Guanajuato's creative essence is reflected in the grandiose Teatro Juárez. This spectacular neoclassical theater, built in the late 1800s, features a horseshoe-shaped auditorium with elaborate plasterwork and gilded accents. Stepping inside seems like entering a bygone period, a tribute to the city's cultural legacy.

A Night at the Theater: I had the opportunity to attend a performance at the Teatro Juárez. The acoustics were perfect, and the mood was fantastic. Watching a performance on this magnificent stage, surrounded by the rich grandeur of the theater, was an unforgettable experience for me. Even if you aren't attending a show, the theater provides guided tours that allow you to go behind the scenes and enjoy the architectural wonder.

Beyond the Stage: The Teatro Juárez is more than just a theatrical space. It's a cultural hub that frequently hosts art exhibitions, film screenings, and other activities. Before you go, check the theater's schedule to see if there is anything that interests you.

Pipila Monument

The Pipila Monument towers above Guanajuato from a magnificent mountaintop. This landmark  honors Juan José Martínez, a youthful soldier known as "El Pípila" who was instrumental in capturing the Alhóndiga de Granaditas during the Mexican War of Independence. El Pípila boldly set fire to the granary entrance, giving the insurgents inside.

A Panoramic View: The monument is a magnificent edifice, but the real prize is the amazing vistas it provides. After ascending the steps or riding the funicular railway, you'll be greeted with a panoramic view of Guanajuato, with colorful dwellings spilling down the slopes. On a clear day, you can see neighboring villages snuggled within the mountains.

A Moment of Reflection: Aside from the breathtaking vistas, the Pipila Monument serves as a striking reminder of the sacrifices made in the war for Mexican independence. Standing at the foot of the monument, looking out at the city below, allows you to connect with the historical significance of this location and appreciate the ongoing spirit of freedom that Guanajuato represents.

These are just a few of the numerous interesting attractions that Guanajuato has to offer. From historical sites to cultural events, the city offers something for everyone. So, put on your walking shoes, embrace your spirit of adventure, and prepare to experience the beauty that awaits you in the heart of Guanajuato.

Exploring Guanajuato City

Guanajuato's enchantment is seen not only in its prominent sites but also in the fabric of its daily existence. This chapter takes you into the city's dynamic center, showing you secret passageways, bustling squares, and architectural marvels.

Walking Tours & City Highlights

While Guanajuato is readily visited on foot, a walking tour provides a unique opportunity to learn about the city's rich history and hidden gems. Local guides, who are passionate about their city, tell stories about Guanajuato's history while pointing out architectural elements that you would miss on your own. I once took part in a historical walking tour that began at the Teatro Cervantes, the city's principal theater. Our guide, Miguel, a captivating storyteller, took us through twisting streets, pausing at each noteworthy sight. He told intriguing stories of the city's silver mining boom, the war for independence, and the lively student culture that defines Guanajuato today. By the end of the tour, I felt as if I had not only seen but also grasped the city's essence.

Beyond the Walking Tour: While walking tours provide a planned experience, don't be afraid to explore alone. Get lost in the maze of cobblestone streets, discover secret plazas filled with colorful fountains, and absorb the city's dynamic spirit. Discovering Guanajuato's hidden gems requires only a handy map and a sense of adventure.

Must-See Highlights: While exploring, be sure to include these prominent places on your schedule.

- **The Jardín de la Unión:** Guanajuato's major plaza, the Jardín de la Unión, is bustling with activity. Street entertainers delight the masses, while cafés provide an opportunity to people-watch and take up the ambiance.
- **Basílica Colegiata de Nuestra Señora de Guanajuato:** The Baroque-style Basílica Colegiata de Nuestra Señora de Guanajuato boasts intricate churrigueresque decoration and is a must-see for architectural enthusiasts.
- **El Mercado Hidalgo:** Immerse yourself in the sights, sounds, and scents of this lively market, which sells everything from local crafts to fresh fruit.

Callejón del Beso (Alley of the Kiss)

In the small Callejón del Beso (Alley of the Kiss), love and folklore interweave. This little passageway is buried in a beautiful tale of two star-crossed lovers who are forbidden by their family to be together. According to legend, if a couple kisses on the third step while standing on opposite sides of the alleyway, their love will be blessed with perpetual happiness.

A Quirky Tradition: I approached the Callejón del Beso with suspicion, yet the atmosphere was appealing. Couples lined up for their chance to kiss, with bystanders cheering them on. Whether or not you believe in the mythology, the Callejón del Beso is a fun experience that reflects the essence of Guanajuato. Just be prepared to wait, particularly during the high tourist season.

Hidden Gems: Although the Callejón del Beso is a major destination, Guanajuato has many more delightful lanes waiting to be discovered. Keep a look out for secret corridors decorated with vivid paintings or leading to unexpected plazas. These hidden jewels provide insight into the city's true nature.

University of Guanajuato.

The University of Guanajuato's young enthusiasm permeates the city. This distinguished school, established in 1822, is located amid a collection of colonial structures, including the unique octagonal Ex-Hacienda de San Gabriel de Barrera, a former hacienda converted into a university building. Walking through the university's courtyards, you'll feel the intellectual bustle and see the city's bustling student life up close.

Beyond the Campus: The University of Guanajuato's reach goes beyond its physical campus. Art exhibitions, theatrical shows, and cultural activities organized by students are common in the city. Attending one of these events is an excellent opportunity to interact with the city's creative energy and gain an understanding of Guanajuato's cultural landscape.

Insider Tip: If you visit Guanajuato during the Cervantino International Festival, which takes place every fall, expect to be amazed by a vivid display of arts and culture. This acclaimed festival draws foreign artists, musicians, and theater companies, converting the city into a showcase for cultural expression.

Colorful Streets & Architecture

Guanajuato's appeal stems not just from its historical sites, but also from its rich colourful hues. Houses painted in every possible color tumble down the slopes, providing a beautiful feast for the eyes. Baroque balconies with elaborate wrought ironwork decorate colonial houses, conveying tales of a bygone period.

A Photographer's Paradise: I spent hours strolling the streets, camera in hand, enthralled by the rainbow of hues. Every bend offered a fresh photo opportunity, from a gateway painted a vivid blue to a street view bathed in the warm glow of a sunset. Guanajuato is a photographers' paradise, with infinite opportunities to capture its particular beauty.

A City that Lives and Breathes: Beyond the aesthetics, Guanajuato's bright streets are alive with activity. Street vendors sell their products, children chase each other across plazas, and the scent of freshly made coffee wafts from cafés. Guanajuato is attractive because of its bright vitality, which invites you to be a part of its continuing tale.

This chapter has just scraped the surface of the many adventures that await you in Guanajuato. So, tie up your walking shoes, enjoy the city's dynamic atmosphere, and prepare to uncover the hidden jewels, dazzling hues, and unmistakable charm that await you around every corner. Guanajuato provides a memorable trip, with history whispering from its walls and magic unfolding with each step.

Cultural Immersion

Guanajuato's beauty extends beyond its cobblestone walkways and lively plazas. The city has a rich cultural heritage woven from creative expression, historical resonance, and dynamic customs. This chapter encourages you to explore the core of Guanajuato's cultural landscape, with activities that will leave you inspired and energized.

Diego Rivera's House Museum

The Diego Rivera House Museum immerses you in the world of one of Mexico's most recognized artists. This museum, located in the muralist's old house, provides insight into Rivera's life and creative process. Wander around the private chambers, filled with his items and sketches, to obtain a better understanding of the artist behind the masterpieces.

A Personal Connection: Going to the Diego Rivera House Museum was a surprise for me; seeing the artist's workstation, his collection of pre-Columbian items, and the bright murals on the walls gave me a new perspective on his creative energy. It wasn't simply the large murals he painted on public buildings; it was his personal life that inspired his creative vision.

Beyond the Walls: The museum also hosts temporary exhibits by other Mexican artists, creating a lively interaction between the past and the present. Check the museum's calendar to see if any special exhibitions overlap with your visit.

Regional Museum of Guanajuato (Alhóndiga de Granaditas).

While we discussed the historical significance of the Alhóndiga de Granaditas in Chapter 3, this magnificent structure provides more than just a look into Mexico's struggle for independence. The Regional Museum of Guanajuato, situated inside its walls, displays a diverse collection of items that illustrate the narrative of the region's cultural legacy.

A Journey Through Time: The museum's displays span centuries, including pre-Hispanic sculptures, colonial art, and ordinary things used throughout history. Walking through the halls will provide you with a better appreciation of the indigenous civilizations that thrived in the region before the advent of the Spanish, the creative influences of the colonial period, and the history of Guanajuato's cultural identity.

Unveiling Local Crafts: A portion of the museum is dedicated to the region's well-known handicrafts. You'll discover beautiful displays of hand-embroidered linens, elegant pottery, and brilliant lacquered artifacts. These handicrafts not only demonstrate the great workmanship of local artists but also provide insight into the region's customs and cultural history.

Festivals & Events

Guanajuato is brimming with vitality all year, featuring a variety of festivals and events celebrating everything from art and culture to history and cuisine.

Cervantino International Festival: The Cervantino International Festival is the indisputable pinnacle of Guanajuato's cultural calendar, taking place every fall. This important festival brings together worldwide performers, musicians, theater groups, and artists, converting the city into a thriving celebration of cultural expression. From street acts and outdoor concerts to opera productions and staged plays, the festival has something for everyone.

Beyond the Cervantino: There are several more festivals and events held in Guanajuato throughout the year. The International Film Festival, held in the spring, features a wide range of independent and international films. The Callejoneadas Festival, held in the summer, fills the streets with the tunes of strolling musicians, creating an enchanting environment. Regardless of when you come, there is sure to be a festival or event that will add vitality to your experience. Tip: Before your trip, check the city's event calendar to see what is scheduled.

Local Art and Craft Markets

Explore Guanajuato's vibrant local markets to get a sense of the city's creative character. These bustling marketplaces are more than simply places to buy souvenirs; they are cultural centers where you can see traditional items being made and interact with local craftsmen.

A Treasure Trove of Creativity: The Mercado Hidalgo is a creative treasure trove that should not be missed by any shopper. This huge market sells everything from handcrafted leather products and colorful linens to locally made pottery and elaborate jewelry. Wander around the aisles, haggle politely with merchants, and find one-of-a-kind items that embody the soul of Guanajuato.

Beyond the Marketplace: Several smaller, more specialized markets cater to certain creative interests. The Ex-Convento Dieguino market is well-known for its collection of handcrafted religious artifacts, whilst the Valenciana market focuses on regional products and traditional sweets. Exploring these little marketplaces provides a fuller understanding of Guanajuato's unique cultural legacy.

A Touch of Local Flavor: While shopping is enjoyable, don't overlook the opportunity to just observe the artists at work. Watch talented potters sculpt clay into intricate designs, listen to the rhythmic tap-tap-tap of a weaver creating a vibrant melody, and admire the passion and craftsmanship that goes into each production. These exchanges provide a look into the heart of Guanajuato's artistic community and foster a stronger connection to the city's cultural essence.

Guanajuato's cultural environment is a rich heritage made from creative expression, historical echoes, and the resilient spirit of its people. From visiting renowned museums to immersing yourself in the spirit of local festivals, the city provides several opportunities to feel its cultural heart.

Hidden Gems & Off the Beaten Path

Beyond the prominent sites and bustling plazas, Guanajuato has a plethora of hidden jewels waiting to be explored. This chapter takes you off the beaten route, introducing you to exciting encounters that reveal the city's lesser-known secrets.

La Valenciana Mine

Visit La Valenciana Mine to learn about Guanajuato's silver mining history. La Valenciana, formerly the wealthiest mine in the Americas, was critical to the city's economic growth. Today, tourists may take a guided trip down into the cold depths of the mine, getting a fascinating peek into the hard working conditions and inventive mining processes used centuries ago.

An Underground Journey: My visit to the La Valenciana Mine was a memorable experience. Walking down the tight tunnels, lit by flickering lamps, I felt like I was transported back in time. The guide told stories of the miners, their difficulties, and the vast treasure retrieved from these depths. Seeing the mining machinery and ruins of the once-thriving enterprise deepened my understanding of the city's historical roots.

Beyond the Mine Shaft: The La Valenciana complex includes a museum that displays mining-related relics such as tools, machinery, historical pictures, and papers. Furthermore, a magnificent vantage point on the site provides spectacular panoramic views of the city and the neighboring mountains.

El Nopal Mine

Consider visiting El Nopal Mine for an even more thrilling adventure. Unlike La Valenciana, El Nopal is an abandoned mine that provides a more raw and untamed experience. Guided excursions are available but prepare for a more difficult journey via tight tunnels and hilly terrain. This event is ideal for folks who enjoy adventure and are naturally curious.

A Step Back in Time: Exploring El Nopal was like walking into the lost past. The abandoned tunnels, which contained pieces of mining carts and gear, provided a disturbing yet oddly compelling peek into the life of the miners who once worked here. This off-the-beaten-path excursion is not for the faint of heart, but it will reward anyone looking for a unique perspective on Guanajuato's mining heritage.

Safety First: When touring El Nopal, make sure to wear sturdy shoes and proper attire. Carefully follow your guide's directions, keeping an eye out for uneven surfaces and low-hanging ceilings.

Secret Gardens & Parks

Escape the city's bustle by visiting Guanajuato's secret gardens and parks. These calm havens provide a welcome change of pace, enabling you to reconnect with nature amidst the cityscape.

The Enchanting Botanica del Carmen: The Botanica del Carmen is an enchanting sanctuary tucked between the walls of a medieval monastery. Wandering around its tranquil courtyards, you'll come across a wide assortment of cactus, succulents, and lush foliage, all expertly organized and perfectly kept. The quiet environment, along with the faint murmur of a nearby fountain, creates an ideal setting for silent contemplation.

A Panoramic View from atop El Pipila: While the Pipila Monument provides beautiful views of the city, continue onward to uncover "El Rincon del pensamiento" (The Thinking Corner), a secluded park. This tranquil refuge, ornamented with sculptures and sheltered by tall trees, offers a panoramic view of the city drenched in golden hues at sunset. It's the ideal location for a quiet period of introspection or a romantic picnic.

Parque Florencio Anza: For a flavor of local life, visit Parque Florencio Anza. This bustling park is popular with families and students. Watch children play on the swings, couples walk hand in hand, and old men converse on park seats. The park also organizes occasional events and concerts, providing insight into the city's thriving social scene.

Lesser-known Museums

Guanajuato's museum culture goes beyond the famed Diego Rivera House Museum and the Regional Museum of Guanajuato. Several smaller, specialty museums explore further into intriguing and frequently unexpected topics.

The Museum of the Mummy of Guanajuato: While the main Mummy Museum has a larger collection, the Museum of the Mummy of Guanajuato focuses on a single, exceptionally well-preserved mummy known as "Juanita." This intimate museum investigates the circumstances surrounding Juanita's mummification and the scientific explanations for the process.

A World of Wax at the Museo Iconográfico de Don Quijote: This one-of-a-kind museum honors Miguel de Cervantes' literary classic Don Quixote and has a collection of life-size wax sculptures recreating scenes from the novel. This interactive experience transports you into the world of Don Quixote and his faithful friend, Sancho Panza.

A Blast from the Past at the Museo Casa Conde Rul: The Museo Casa Conde Rul is a must-see for history aficionados. This museum, located in a magnificently maintained 18th-century home, displays furniture, clothes, and everyday artifacts used by the city's aristocratic people during the colonial period. Wandering around the large chambers provides an insight into the lavish lifestyle of Guanajuato's aristocracy.

Discovering Guanajuato's hidden jewels is like going on a treasure hunt. From exploring old mines to finding peace in calm gardens, these off-the-beaten-path activities provide a deeper connection with the city's essence. So embrace your spirit of adventure, pursue your curiosity, and uncover the hidden charm of Guanajuato.

Day Trips from Guanajuato

Guanajuato's appeal goes beyond its city borders. The surrounding area has a plethora of intriguing sites ideal for a day trip. This chapter takes you beyond the city limits, showing you lovely communities, historical sites, and stunning natural beauty.

San Miguel de Allende

Explore San Miguel de Allende, a UNESCO World Heritage Site known for its colonial architecture and strong creative atmosphere. San Miguel, approximately an hour's drive from Guanajuato, is an art lover's paradise, with various galleries, studios, and a well-known Fine Arts School.

Wandering through San Miguel de Allende's cobblestoned streets is a sensory experience. The plazas are lined with baroque facades painted in vivid hues, and the fragrance of freshly baked products wafts from attractive cafés. Street musicians fill the air with music, and artists showcase their wares in bustling marketplaces.

Must-Sees in San Miguel: Begin your journey at the famed Parroquia de San Miguel Arcángel, a stunning pink sandstone church known for its intricate neo gothic spires. The La Casa del Mayorazgo Museum explores Mexican modernism, while the Museo Histórico Casa de Ignacio Allende commemorates the life of the independence hero.

Explore beyond the central area to find hidden jewels such as the Fábrica La Aurora, a former textile mill that has been turned into a bustling arts and cultural center. For a natural experience, visit the picturesque overlook at El Charco del Ingenio, which provides panoramic views of the surrounding area.

Tip: San Miguel de Allende is a popular tourist destination, particularly on weekends and holidays. Consider going on a weekday for a more calm atmosphere.

Dolores Hidalgo

Travel back in time to Dolores Hidalgo, the birthplace of Mexico's struggle for independence. This lovely village, located approximately an hour from Guanajuato, was instrumental in sparking the revolution.

On September 16, 1810, Miguel Hidalgo y Costilla, a Catholic priest, uttered the now-famous "Grito de

Dolores" (Cry of Dolores) from the balcony of the Parroquia de Nuestra Señora de las Dolores, sparking the rebellion. This passionate appeal to arms signaled the start of Mexico's war for independence from Spanish domination.

Exploring Dolores Hidalgo: Visit the Casa Museo Miguel Hidalgo, the revolutionary priest's old house that has been converted into a museum depicting his life and the events leading up to the Grito de Dolores. The old Parroquia, where Hidalgo gave his famous address, is another must-see. Take a moment to stand on the exact balcony that saw this watershed event in Mexican history.

Beyond History: Dolores Hidalgo provides more than just a historical experience. The lively Mercado Hidalgo is an excellent spot to buy local crafts and experience delectable regional dishes. Furthermore, the town is well-known for its handcrafted celadon ceramics, making it an ideal destination for anyone looking for a one-of-a-kind memento.

Mineral de Pozos

Mineral de Pozos is a fascinating community where you may experience the unexpected. This old mining town, approximately an hour and a half from Guanajuato, has a distinctive blend of abandoned mineshafts, colonial buildings, and a thriving creative community.

A Reclaimed Town: Mineral de Pozos, once a prosperous mining community, declined as the silver mines were drained. However, in recent years, the town has seen a renaissance, drawing artists, businesspeople, and visitors looking for a one-of-a-kind experience.

Exploring the Past: Visit the abandoned Molino Mina San Bernabé, a former mill that has been converted into a cultural center, to learn about the area's mining history. Take a guided journey into the depths of a nearby mine to see the brutal realities of miners' existence.

Mineral de Pozos' modern art scene is thriving. Wander along the small alleyways, pausing to visit art galleries built in old haciendas or converted shops. On weekends, the main square comes alive with a local artist market, allowing visitors to explore unique items while also supporting local artists.

Tip: Mineral de Pozos is noted for its daring activities, such as rappelling down abandoned mine shafts. If you're searching for a thrill, book one of these trips from a reliable company.

Sierra de Santa Rosa

Escape the city and immerse yourself in the natural splendor of the Sierra de Santa Rosa. This mountain range, just outside of Guanajuato, provides a paradise for outdoor enthusiasts and environment lovers.

Hike across magnificent routes, breathe in the fresh mountain air, and see the rich flora and wildlife. A hot air balloon flight above the beautiful peaks provides a unique perspective and panoramic views of the surrounding countryside.

A Sanctuary for Adventure: The Sierra de Santa Rosa welcomes adventurers of all levels. Experienced hikers can take on hard treks such as the one leading to the peak of El Cubre, the region's highest point. For a more leisurely experience, horseback riding trips provide a lovely opportunity to explore the highlands.

A Hidden Gem: Nestled inside the Sierra de Santa Rosa is the ***Presa de la Olla***, a man-made reservoir surrounded by luxuriant flora. This peaceful location is ideal for a picnic lunch, a relaxing dip in the calm waters, or simply taking in the beauty of nature.

Beyond the Mountains: The Sierra de Santa Rosa area has several historical and cultural attractions. The Sanctuary of Cristo Rey, a huge Christ the Redeemer monument set on a mountaintop, provides stunning vistas and a calm space for reflection. Furthermore, the lovely community of Mineral de Cata has a rich mining history and is famous for its homemade cheese, making it a wonderful stop on your day trip.

Whether you're looking for cultural immersion, a historical adventure, or a taste of natural beauty, going outside Guanajuato City opens up a world of interesting activities. So, pack your day bag, embrace your spirit of adventure, and discover the hidden beauties of the countryside around this dynamic and ancient city.

Culinary Delights

Guanajuato's beauty extends well beyond its cobblestone walkways and vibrant architecture. This dynamic city has a rich culinary tradition, providing a delectable journey for all tastes. This chapter goes into the heart of Guanajuato's food culture, introducing you to classic delicacies, hidden jewels, and memorable gastronomic experiences.

Traditional Guanajuato Cuisine

Guanajuato's cuisine is a savory expression of the region's rich history and cultural variety. Traditional recipes here are a harmonic combination of indigenous ingredients and Spanish influences, resulting in a distinctive culinary heritage. Some of the must-try traditional dishes are:

- **Enchiladas Mineras:** Inspired by the mining tradition, these enchiladas are packed with cheese and onions, covered with a red chili sauce, and served with potatoes and carrots.

- **Fiambre:** A colorful salad with meats, vegetables, and fruits that is frequently served during special events and festivals.
- **Gorditas:** Thick corn cakes loaded with beans, cheese, or chicharrón (pork rinds).
- **Nopalitos:** Nopalitos are tender cactus paddles used in salads, stews, and as a side dish.
- **Cajeta:** A delicious caramel sauce prepared with goat's milk that is commonly used in pastries.

Each meal offers a tale about Guanajuato's history, from its indigenous beginnings to its colonial influences, and it's a delightful way to learn about the region's legacy.

Best Restaurants and Eateries

Guanajuato has a wide range of dining alternatives, from expensive restaurants to quaint local cafes. Here are some of the greatest venues to enjoy local cuisine:

- **Casa Valadez:** Located near the Teatro Juárez, this exquisite restaurant provides a superb dining experience with a menu that includes both traditional Mexican specialties and foreign cuisine.

- **Los Campos:** This restaurant is popular with both residents and guests due to its warm ambiance and unique spins on classic Mexican meals.
- **Mestizo:** This trendy restaurant specializes in innovative Mexican food made with fresh, local ingredients. The tasting menu is a gourmet experience worth taking.
- **El Midi Bistro:** With a menu combining Mexican and Mediterranean cuisines, El Midi Bistro is ideal for those seeking a casual lunch in a sophisticated environment.
- **Truco 7:** A popular restaurant housed in an ancient colonial house, recognized for its hearty traditional meals and attractive atmosphere.

Whether you want a sophisticated experience or a simple lunch, these restaurants represent the finest of Guanajuato's culinary scene.

Street Food Adventures

Nothing compares to Guanajuato's robust street food scene. Street sellers sell a range of delectable foods that are both tasty and inexpensive. Here are some popular street foods to try:

- **Tacos al Pastor:** Marinated pork tacos served with pineapple, cilantro, and onions, usually with a squeeze of lime and a sprinkle of salsa.
- **Elotes & Esquites:** Grilled corn on the cob (elotes) or corn kernels in a cup (esquites), sometimes served with mayonnaise, cheese, chili powder, and lime.
- **Gorditas:** Small stuffed maize cakes loaded with delicious ingredients such as beans, cheese, or meats that are commonly consumed as a quick and enjoyable snack.
- **Tamales:** Corn dough stuffed with meats, cheeses, or vegetables, covered in corn husks, and steamed until perfect.
- **Buñuelos:** Buñuelos are crispy, sweet fritters dusted with sugar or drizzled with syrup that fulfill your sweet craving.

One of my favorite street food experiences in Guanajuato was at a local market, when I ate a platter of sizzling hot churros, crispy on the exterior and soft on the inside, accompanied with a thick chocolate dipping sauce. The blend of tastes and textures was just delicious.

Food Festivals

Guanajuato's food festivals are lively celebrations of the region's gastronomic heritage, with visitors able to enjoy a variety of traditional dishes and local delicacies. Some of the most renowned culinary festivals are

Festival de la Cocina Tradicional: This event celebrates traditional Mexican food via culinary demonstrations, tastings, and workshops. This is an excellent opportunity to learn about Guanajuato's culinary heritage.

Festival Internacional Cervantino: While the Cervantino is primarily an arts festival, it also includes a broad range of food vendors serving anything from street cuisine to gourmet delicacies, creating a gastronomic experience that complements the artistic events.

Feria de la Alfeñique y Dulce Tradicional: Celebrate traditional sweets and confections including sugar skulls and marzipan figurines for the Day of the Dead.

Event del Mole: This event honors one of Mexico's most famous sauces, celebrating the rich and complex flavors of mole with a variety of regional versions available for tasting.

Attending these events is an excellent chance to immerse yourself in local culture, meet brilliant chefs and craftsmen, and sample some of Guanajuato's greatest cuisine.

Finally, Guanajuato's gastronomic pleasures are a feast for the senses, providing a wide range of sensations and experiences. From classic delicacies rooted in history to current culinary inventions, the region's food culture is likely to make an indelible impact on every visitor. Whether dining at a high-end restaurant, sampling street cuisine, or visiting a colorful food festival, Guanajuato's culinary experiences are as memorable as they are tasty.

Nightlife & Entertainment

As the sun sets, Guanajuato changes into a city with a thriving nightlife. Cobblestone streets pulsate with vitality, inviting you to explore its pubs, music venues, and cultural acts to suit any taste. This chapter goes into the core of Guanajuato's nightlife culture, providing a tour of the city's nighttime offers.

Best Bars & Pubs

Guanajuato's nightlife is a lovely blend of intimate bars, vibrant pubs, and distinctive venues, each with its personality and charm. Here are some of the top spots to spend a night out in the city:

Bar Fly: A famous rooftop bar known for its laid-back vibe and spectacular views over Guanajuato's cityscape. It's a nice place to relax with a beverage and watch the sunset.

El Incendio: This trendy bar serves a wide variety of craft beers and imaginative drinks. The vivid design and live DJ performances make it popular among both residents and visitors.

La Ingrata: With its rustic design and laid-back feel, La Ingrata is ideal for those seeking a more relaxed evening. The bar has an excellent assortment of local beers and spirits.

Los Lobos: Known for its unique blend of music and bohemian ambiance, Los Lobos is a nice area to have a drink and some excellent company.

Cervecería del Truco: This microbrewery serves locally made beers and great pub cuisine. It's an excellent venue to try some of Guanajuato's finest artisan beers.

Each of these clubs and pubs offers a distinct experience of Guanajuato's dynamic nightlife, guaranteeing that there is something for everyone.

Live Music & Dance Venues

Music and dance are vital parts of Guanajuato's cultural fabric, and the city comes alive at night with a variety of venues hosting live performances. Whether you prefer traditional Mexican music, rock, jazz, or salsa, you'll find a spot to do it here.

Zilch Bar: This club is well-known for its live rock and indie acts. The compact atmosphere enables close-up interactions with both local and touring musicians.

Bar Ocho: Known for its vibrant environment and eclectic music options, Bar Ocho usually offers live salsa bands, making it a popular place to dance the night away.

El Club de la Bohemia: This club is a hotspot for jazz fans, with frequent concerts by outstanding local and international artists. The easygoing atmosphere and outstanding acoustics make it a favorite among jazz enthusiasts.

El Dada: This unique pub showcases a range of live music performances ranging from folk to techno, resulting in a diverse and ever-changing experience.

Callejón del Beso: A prominent landmark that also hosts impromptu street acts. Musicians and dancers frequently meet here, creating a spontaneous and real entertainment experience.

Live music and dance in Guanajuato are a must-see, providing a glimpse into the city's vibrant cultural landscape.

Nighttime Cultural Performances

Guanajuato's rich cultural past is on full display in its nocturnal festivities, which include theater, traditional music, and dance. Here are a few highlights.

Teatro Juárez: One of the city's most recognizable monuments, this theater showcases a wide range of acts, including classical music concerts, operas, and traditional Mexican folk plays. Its towering architecture and lavish decor enhance the enchanting experience of a night at the theater.

Callejoneadas: A distinct Guanajuato custom, these musical walking excursions are conducted by local musicians dressed in traditional clothing. As they lead you through the small streets and alleyways, they sing, play instruments, and tell local tales, creating a magical and engaging atmosphere.

Cervantino Festival: The Festival Internacional Cervantino takes place every October and is one of Latin America's most major cultural events. It presents a diverse spectrum of acts, including theater, dance, music, and visual arts. Even when the festival isn't going on, Guanajuato's thriving cultural community keeps things interesting.

Attending these cultural acts immerses you in Guanajuato's creative essence, giving you a better understanding of the region's traditions and inventiveness.

Guanajuato at Night

Guanajuato changes at night, with lit streets and antique structures throwing a lovely glow over the city. Here are several ways to enjoy Guanajuato at night:

Nighttime Strolls: The city's colonial architecture and tiny lanes are especially beautiful at night. A stroll around the old district, passing attractions such as the Basilica of Our Lady of Guanajuato and the Teatro Juárez, displays the city's splendor in a new light.

El Pipila Monument: The El Pipila Monument offers sweeping views of the city's evening skyline. The monument is spectacular, and the vantage point provides stunning views of the lit town.

Square de la Paz: This major square comes alive at night with street performers, merchants, and people taking in the crisp evening air. It's an excellent area to people-watch and absorb the local ambiance.

Restaurants with Views: Many Guanajuato restaurants provide rooftop dining, which allows you to enjoy spectacular views of the city while you eat. The mix of good cuisine and a stunning background creates an unforgettable dining experience.

Guanajuato at night is a unique experience that combines historical charm with exciting nightlife, making your evenings as unforgettable as your days.

Outdoor Activities

Guanajuato is not just a city with a rich history and lively culture; it is also a destination for outdoor enthusiasts. Beyond the crowded plazas and tiny streets, there are rolling hills, magnificent mountain ranges, and verdant valleys to explore. This chapter encourages you to leave the city boundaries and enjoy the fresh air, stunning views, and exciting experiences that Guanajuato's natural beauty provides.

Hikes and Nature Trails

Guanajuato's diversified geography provides a wealth of hiking and nature routes suitable for both casual walkers and experienced hikers. The city's surroundings are characterized by undulating hills, spectacular gorges, and lush woods, making it an excellent choice for outdoor enthusiasts.

One of the most popular hikes is the trek to the **Sierra de Santa Rosa**, a mountain range located just outside the city. This region has a network of paths that go through pine forests, past quiet lakes, and lead to picturesque vistas. The paths vary in complexity, so there's something for everyone. The modest trek to **Peña de Bernal** provides spectacular vistas and opportunities to observe local wildlife, including many bird species.

Another must-see destination is the **Grutas de San Bernardo**, a system of caves located just outside Guanajuato. The trip to the caverns is reasonably straightforward and ideal for families. The trail winds through picturesque farmland, and the caverns themselves offer a cool relief from the heat, with spectacular stalactites and stalagmites to admire.

For those wishing to mix history with hiking, the **El Cerro del Cubilete trek** is an excellent choice. This route leads to the Christ the King statue, which is one of Mexico's most prominent religious monuments. The climb is strenuous yet rewarding, providing panoramic views of the area and insight into the country's cultural legacy.

Bike Routes

Biking across Guanajuato is an excellent way to discover the region's natural beauty and vibrant communities. The varied terrain provides routes for all ability levels, from relaxing rides to tough mountain bike tracks.

The Camino Real de Tierra Adentro is a historic highway that previously connected Mexico City and Santa Fe. Today, it serves as a lovely bicycling track that winds through charming villages and undulating hills. The route is mainly flat, making it suitable for all skill levels, and it offers an excellent opportunity to learn about the region's history and surroundings.

For those looking for more of a challenge, the *Presa de la Olla* region has difficult mountain bike paths that snake through deep forests and along the edge of stunning cliffs. These trails are ideal for experienced cyclists seeking an adrenaline rush and stunning scenery. *The Ruta de la Plata*, or Silver Route, is another wonderful option. This route takes you into the heart of Guanajuato's mining sector, using a combination of paved highways and dirt paths of moderate difficulty. Its historical significance and geographical beauty make it a popular destination for local bikers.

Renting a bike in Guanajuato is simple, with several outlets providing rentals and guided trips. One of my most memorable bike rides was a guided tour of the *Bocamina San Ramón mine*. The track combined historical research with natural beauty, culminating in an exciting drop into the heart of the mining district.

Horseback Riding.

Horseback riding in Guanajuato is a fun way to explore the countryside and appreciate the area's natural beauty. Several ranches and tour providers offer guided horseback riding trips for riders of all skill levels.

Rancho Xotolar, located just outside of San Miguel de Allende, is a famous horseback riding location. The ranch provides guided trips via spectacular scenery such as canyons, rivers, and wide plains. The educated guides educate visitors about the local flora and animals, as well as the area's history.

In the ***Sierra de Guanajuato***, you may go horseback riding along wooded routes and to picturesque views. These trips frequently include a picnic or BBQ, allowing you to enjoy a meal while admiring the spectacular environment. ***La Hacienda San Gabriel de Barrera*** is another great place for horseback riding. This ancient house provides guided rides around the wonderfully manicured gardens and neighboring countryside.

It's an excellent opportunity to mix outdoor activities with a little history.

During my horseback riding tour in Guanajuato, I was surprised by how peaceful it was. Riding across the wide countryside, with the sound of hooves and the aroma of wildflowers in the air, was a relaxing and wonderful experience.

Parks & Gardens

Guanajuato's parks and gardens give tranquil respites from the city's hectic streets, with lush green places for relaxing, picnicking, and enjoying nature.

The Jardín de la Unión is the center of Guanajuato's social scene. This attractive garden, located in the city center, is flanked by old buildings and shaded by big Indian laurels. It's an ideal place to relax and people-watch, get a coffee from a neighboring café, or listen to the local mariachi bands who frequently perform here.

The Parque Florencio Antillón offers a larger green space. This park, near the Presa de la Olla, has walking pathways, playgrounds, and picnic spots. It's an ideal location for a stroll or a family trip. The park is particularly attractive in the early morning when the light is gentle and the air is fresh.

The Jardín Botánico El Charco del Ingenio in San Miguel de Allende is a must-see for plant lovers. This botanical garden focuses on the preservation of Mexican vegetation, notably cacti and succulents. The garden's enormous collection and picturesque setting make it an ideal day excursion from Guanajuato.

Finally, **the Parque Bicentenario** provides a variety of recreational and cultural attractions. This contemporary park features recreational facilities, strolling pathways, and a small museum. It's an excellent area to spend the day exploring nature and local history.

In Conclusion, Guanajuato's outdoor activities provide a wide variety of adventures, including hiking, bicycling, horseback riding, and touring gorgeous parks and gardens. Whether you choose action or relaxation, the region's natural beauty and rich history have something for everyone.

Shopping & Souvenirs

Guanajuato is more than simply a sensory delight; it is also a treasure hunter's heaven. Beyond its ancient landmarks and rich culture, there is a treasure mine of unusual items just waiting to be discovered. This chapter goes into the heart of Guanajuato's retail scene, bringing you through crowded markets, quaint shops, and the best locations to discover original gifts that will transport you back home with a bit of the city's romance.

Artisan Markets

Guanajuato's artisan markets are a colorful representation of the area's rich cultural history and workmanship. These lively markets are ideal for finding one-of-a-kind, handcrafted products that exemplify Guanajuato culture.

Mercado Hidalgo: Located in the center of Guanajuato City, Mercado Hidalgo is a treasure trove of locally sourced items. This old market, situated in a large iron edifice, sells a wide range of things, including fresh vegetables, spices, handcrafted crafts, and souvenirs. The colorful environment and courteous merchants make shopping here an enjoyable experience.

Mercado de Artesanías: A short walk from the city center, this market specializes in artisanal products. There are a variety of products available, including colorful fabrics, ceramics, jewelry, and leather goods. The quality and diversity of crafts available make it a must-see for anybody wishing to take home a piece of Guanajuato's artistic legacy.

Square de la Paz: During weekends and festivals, this major square changes into a thriving artisan market. Local artists and crafters set up stalls to sell their creations, ranging from hand-painted pottery to beautifully woven baskets.

Exploring these markets is more than simply buying; it's an opportunity to learn about the local culture and engage with the craftspeople who keep these traditions alive.

Local Boutiques

Guanajuato's lovely boutiques provide a carefully chosen range of high-quality products ranging from clothes and accessories to home decor. These businesses provide a more personal shopping experience, frequently featuring the work of local designers and craftspeople.

Casa Cuatro: Located in San Miguel de Allende, this store is well-known for its fashion and accessories. The store combines contemporary and traditional styles, with a focus on locally produced materials and ecological procedures.

Artesanías El Vuelo: This business offers handmade crafts and ornamental things. From hand-carved wooden sculptures to exquisitely made fabrics, each piece showcases the skill and creativity of local artists.

La Calaca: A prominent store in Guanajuato City that sells unusual gifts and souvenirs. The business is well renowned for its Day of the Dead merchandise, which includes painted skulls and papier-mâché figurines.

Shopping at these shops is a great opportunity to find unique goods while also supporting local artists and designers.

Traditional Crafts

Guanajuato is well-known for its traditional crafts, which represent the region's long history and cultural variety. These crafts are frequently created utilizing skills passed down through generations, resulting in exquisitely produced and culturally valuable artifacts.

Talavera Pottery: This unusual form of pottery, with its complex designs and brilliant colors, is a symbol of Mexican workmanship. Talavera plates, vases, and tiles make excellent decorative items and mementos.

Textiles: Handwoven textiles are an important craft in Guanajuato. These textiles, ranging from vibrant rebozos (shawls) to beautifully embroidered apparel, are created utilizing ancient processes and natural dyes.

Leather Goods: The region is also well known for producing high-quality leather items like purses, belts, and shoes. These goods are made with great care and durability, making them both functional and fashionable mementos.

One of my favorite purchases in Guanajuato was a hand-painted Talavera plate. Every time I see it, I am reminded of the region's rich cultural legacy by its brilliant colors and detailed design.

Top Places to Buy Souvenirs

Finding the ideal gift in Guanajuato is a fascinating experience, with several stores and marketplaces giving a diverse range of possibilities. Here are some of the top places to buy souvenirs:

La Casa del Quijote: This store sells a variety of traditional Mexican goods such as pottery, textiles, and jewelry. It's an excellent site to get genuine, high-quality souvenirs.

Galería La Compañía: Located in San Miguel de Allende, this gallery showcases local artists and crafters. The assortment includes paintings, sculptures, and decorative items, making it an excellent place to find one-of-a-kind creative mementos.

Museo del Pueblo de Guanajuato: The gift store of this museum has a well-chosen assortment of crafts and publications about the region's history and culture. It's a great place to get educated and culturally valuable souvenirs.

Tianguis de los Mártires: Held on weekends, this open-air market is a lively and busy spot to browse for gifts. The market sells a broad variety of items, from handcrafted crafts to antiques and treasures.

When shopping for souvenirs, keep in mind that the finest goods almost always come with a narrative. Taking the time to learn about the products and the craftsmen who make them adds a personal touch to your purchases and enhances your vacation experience.

To summarize, shopping in Guanajuato is more than simply a retail experience; it is an exploration of the region's creative and cultural legacy. From lively markets and quaint shops to traditional crafts and one-of-a-kind souvenirs, every purchase captures a bit of Guanajuato's colorful spirit. Whether you're searching for a souvenir to commemorate your vacation or a particular gift for someone back home, Guanajuato's shopping experiences will leave you with lasting memories and treasures.

Family-Friendly Activities

Guanajuato is a wonderful family vacation location, with a wide range of activities suitable for all ages. Everyone may find something to enjoy, from interactive museums and large parks to interesting excursions and wildlife encounters.

Child-Friendly Museums

Museums in Guanajuato are not limited to adults. Many of them contain displays and activities geared toward engaging youngsters and making learning enjoyable.

Museo de las Momias: Although it may seem creepy, the Mummy Museum is an intriguing site for children who like the macabre and strange. The museum displays a collection of naturally mummified remains, which provide a unique peek into the past. It's a one-of-a-kind educational experience, complete with interactive displays and explanations for children. I recall going with my children and witnessing their wide-eyed enthusiasm as they learned about the history and science of mummification.

Museo del Juguete Popular Mexicano: This museum houses a vast collection of traditional Mexican toys. Children may see and even play with some of the toys, learning about their cultural values and history. The bright and imaginative exhibits entice young visitors, making it an enjoyable trip for families.

Museo de Historia Natural Alfredo Dugès: Located in the University of Guanajuato, this natural history museum houses a variety of exhibits on local flora and animals. The dinosaur skeletons and taxidermied creatures are always popular with children. I remember my son's enthusiasm when he saw a massive dinosaur skeleton towering over him, prompting a spirited debate about prehistoric species.

Parks & Playgrounds

Outdoor places in Guanajuato offer several options for families to rest and play. The city's parks and playgrounds are ideal for a day of family activities.

Parque Guanajuato Bicentenario: This big park has a range of leisure activities, such as bike routes, playgrounds, and picnic spots. The park also has an educational component with its science and technology exhibits. During a family visit, we had a leisurely bike ride followed by lunch beneath the trees, making for a lovely day out.

Parque Florencio Antillón: Located near the Presa de la Olla, this park is ideal for family outings. It has a huge playground, strolling routes, and open areas for children to run and play. The neighboring lake is ideal for a stroll, and you could even come across a local festival or event.

Jardín de la Unión: A town plaza with cafés and restaurants, this garden is ideal for families to relax. The center fountain and shaded seats provide an ideal spot for a respite, and street performers frequently amuse pedestrians, much to the joy of youngsters.

Family Tours & Activities

Exploring Guanajuato with your family may be an experience in itself. Several trips and activities are created exclusively for families.

Callejoneadas: These musical walking tours provide a unique and fascinating way to explore Guanajuato's small streets and alleyways. The tours, guided by local musicians dressed in traditional garb, include music, anecdotes, and intriguing facts about the city. Our family attended a Callejoneada one evening, and the kids enjoyed singing and dancing to the upbeat music.

El Cubilete: Visiting the Cristo Rey monument on El Cubilete mountain provides both a spiritual and exciting experience. The drive up the mountain provides amazing vistas, as does the site itself. Our children liked the climb up, and we were all impressed by the panoramic views from the summit.

La Mina de Valenciana: Visiting the Valenciana Mine provides insight into Guanajuato's rich mining history. Guided tours take families into the subterranean tunnels, explaining the mining process and its importance in the region. My children were enthralled by the stories of miners and the opportunity to see a real mine.

Zoos and Aquariums

Children are often fascinated by animal encounters, and Guanajuato offers a few places where families can get up close and personal with nature.

Zoo León: Located near León, this zoo is a popular family attraction. It is home to a diverse range of creatures, including large cats, monkeys, reptiles, and birds. The zoo also has a petting area where children may engage with domesticated animals. During our visit, my daughter was ecstatic to feed a giraffe, which she still speaks about.

Acuario del Bajío: This aquarium in León provides an exciting underwater environment for children to explore. With tanks full of colorful fish, sea turtles, and other aquatic life, it's a fascinating experience for people of all ages. Interactive displays and feeding presentations add to the thrill, and our family thoroughly enjoyed learning about many marine animals together.

Parque Zoológico de Irapuato: Another excellent choice for animal enthusiasts, this zoo has a diverse range of animals and is noted for its well-kept grounds and family-friendly environment. The butterfly garden was a pleasure for us, and our children loved walking amid hundreds of butterflies.

Guanajuato boasts a plethora of activities suitable for families, guaranteeing that every member, young and old, has a fun and unforgettable time. The city offers several options for entertainment, education, and adventure, including interactive museums and wide parks, as well as interesting excursions and wildlife encounters. Family-friendly activities in Guanajuato will leave you with lasting memories, whether you're visiting ancient places, having a fun day in the park, or marveling at the beauty of nature.

Travel Tips & Safety

Guanajuato is a beautiful and culturally rich location, but like with any travel experience, you must be prepared and educated. This chapter contains crucial suggestions for a safe and pleasurable journey, including health measures, navigation, local traditions, and emergency services.

Health & Safety Precautions

Traveling with health and safety in mind is critical for a stress-free holiday. Here are some important safeguards to follow.

Stay Hydrated: Guanajuato's weather may be hot, especially during the summer months. To keep hydrated, always carry a water bottle. Bottled water is preferred over tap water to avoid gastrointestinal problems.

Dish Safety: When eating local cuisine, be sure the dish is well prepared and served hot. Street food is an enjoyable aspect of the Guanajuato experience; however, seek busy vendors, as high turnover frequently equals fresher food.

Sun Protection: Because of the high altitude, the sun is more direct. Wear sunscreen, a hat, and sunglasses to protect your skin from the sun. Reapply sunscreen frequently, especially if you will be outside for a lengthy amount of time.

Medical Supplies: Bring a basic first-aid kit, including bandages, antiseptic wipes, and any personal prescriptions. Pharmacies are commonly available, however, keeping basic supplies on hand is always beneficial.

Vaccines: Make sure your usual vaccines are up to date. Consult a healthcare practitioner about any extra immunizations required for travel to Mexico.

Navigating the City

Guanajuato's lovely but winding alleys may be both captivating and perplexing. Here are some suggestions to help you move around:

Walking: Most of Guanajuato's attractions are within walking distance of one another. The city's small, twisting lanes are best explored on foot. Wear comfortable shoes, as certain places may be steep and uneven.

Public Transportation: Buses are an economical method to go about the city and to neighboring cities. Learn a few main roads or ask locals for directions. Guanajuato's major bus terminal, Central de Autobuses, connects the city with the rest of the area.

Taxis & Ride Sharing: Taxis are easily accessible and reasonably priced. Before beginning your journey, make sure the taxi is registered and runs on a meter, or agree on a rate. Ride-sharing applications such as Uber also exist and offer a handy option.

Tunnels: Guanajuato is well-known for its extensive network of subterranean tunnels that assist regulate traffic and connect various regions of the city. These tunnels might be complicated, so if you're driving, a GPS can be really useful.

Local Etiquette & Customs

Understanding local customs and etiquette may improve your travel experience and allow you to interact with locals.

Greetings: Use cordial greetings, such as "Hola" or "Buenos días" (Good morning). Mexicans frequently greet one another with a handshake or a kiss on the cheek, depending on their level of acquaintance.

Politeness: Politeness is an essential aspect of Mexican culture. Always use "por favor" (please) and "gracias" (thank you). Using "Señor" (Mr.), "Señora" (Mrs.), or "Señorita" (Miss) to address someone demonstrates respect.

Punctuality: Although Mexicans are known for their laid-back attitude toward time, it is vital to arrive on time for formal occasions or business meetings. Arriving late to social engagements is typically acceptable.

Dress Code: Be modest, particularly while visiting religious locations. Shorts and sleeveless shirts may be appropriate in tourist destinations, but conservative clothing is preferable in churches and other traditional situations.

Tipping: Tipping is traditional in Mexico. In restaurants, a tip of 10-15% is expected. Bellboys and housekeepers get minor gratuities from hotel guests. Taxi drivers seldom seek gratuities, but rounding up the fare is a lovely gesture.

Emergency Contacts & Services

Knowing who to contact in case of an emergency is critical to your safety and peace of mind.

Emergency Numbers: In Mexico, the basic emergency number is 911. This will allow you to contact police, fire, and medical services.

Embassy: In the event of a major emergency, the nearest embassy or consulate might be an invaluable resource. The United States Consulate in León, for example, covers Guanajuato and can help with lost passports, legal concerns, and other urgent situations.

Local Authorities: The Policía Turística (Tourist Police) are trained to help travelers. They can give directions, assist with misplaced objects, and maintain public safety in famous tourist destinations.

Hospitals & Clinics: Become acquainted with the nearby hospital or clinic. *Hospital General de Guanajuato* and *Hospital Médica San Gabriel* are well-known medical institutions in the city. For mild illnesses, pharmacies frequently employ a resident pharmacist who may offer guidance and over-the-counter drugs.

To summarize, Guanajuato is a pleasant and reasonably secure place, although it is always advisable to travel prepared. You may ensure a smooth and pleasurable vacation by following health and safety measures, learning how to traverse the city, respecting local customs, and having emergency contacts. Whether you're strolling through the attractive streets, enjoying local food, or conversing with the friendly inhabitants, being knowledgeable and prepared can help you make the most of your stay in this lovely city.

Sustainable & Responsible Travel

Traveling sustainably and ethically in Guanajuato not only helps to conserve the environment but also benefits local people and guarantees that future generations may appreciate the beauty and culture of this dynamic region. This chapter offers practical advice on eco-friendly activities, community service, lowering your carbon impact, and ethical souvenir buying.

Eco-Friendly Activities

Engaging in eco-friendly activities allows you to appreciate Guanajuato's natural beauty while reducing your environmental effects.

Hiking & Nature Walks: Exploring the Sierra de Santa Rosa's nature paths is an excellent opportunity to get to know the local flora and animals. Trails like "El Cerro de la Bufa" provide beautiful vistas and the opportunity to interact with nature. Remember to follow indicated pathways to safeguard native ecosystems.

Cycling Excursions: Consider guided bicycle excursions, which not only give an active way to explore the sites but also lessen dependency on fossil fuels. Many excursions focus on the region's natural and cultural assets, giving visitors a better knowledge of the place.

Bird Watching: Guanajuato is home to a diverse range of bird species. Participate in bird-watching trips that support conservation initiatives. These trips are frequently guided by skilled guides who provide insights into local species and environments.

Eco-Friendly Accommodation: Select hotels and accommodations that use sustainable methods including solar energy, recycling programs, and water conservation measures. Casa Estrella de la Valenciana is well-known for its environmentally friendly activities.

Supporting Local Communities

Supporting local communities preserves Guanajuato's distinct culture while also providing economic advantages to its citizens.

Buy Local: Support local businesses by purchasing goods and services. Whether you eat at a family-owned restaurant or buy handcrafted items from local craftsmen, your purchases directly benefit the community.

Stay Local: Choose locally owned lodgings, such as bed & breakfasts or small boutique hotels. These enterprises frequently give a more customized experience while also keeping money inside the neighborhood.

Cultural Excursions: Participate in excursions and activities led by locals. This not only offers an authentic experience but also helps to support local livelihoods. Consider attending cooking lessons, historical walking tours, or craft workshops.

Volunteer Opportunities: Participate in volunteer projects that assist the community. Giving back while traveling may take various forms, from teaching English to local youngsters to engaging in environmental conservation programs.

Reducing Your Carbon Footprint

Traveling responsibly entails making thoughtful decisions to reduce your environmental effects. Here are some ways to lower your carbon impact when visiting Guanajuato.

Transportation Options: Instead of hiring a car, take public transportation, ride a bike, or walk. Guanajuato's tight city center is ideal for exploring on foot, and taking buses or ride-sharing services for larger distances may drastically lessen your carbon footprint.

Energy Conservation: Be conscious of your energy consumption in hotels. When you are not using lights, air conditioning, or devices, turn them off. Many hotels now allow guests to reuse towels and bed sheets, saving water and electricity.

Water Usage: Water is a valuable resource. Take shorter showers, avoid doing superfluous laundry, and utilize water-saving gadgets when available. In areas like Guanajuato, where water is limited, every drop matters.

Sustainable Eating: Eating locally and seasonally can help you reduce your carbon footprint. This not only benefits local farmers but also saves energy when shipping food across great distances. Many restaurants in Guanajuato deliver wonderful meals produced using locally sourced ingredients.

Ethical Souvenir Shopping

Purchasing souvenirs is a terrific way to remember your vacation, but you should purchase ethically and sustainably.

Local & Handmade: Choose items manufactured locally. This benefits craftsmen and keeps traditional crafts alive. Look for marketplaces like Mercado Hidalgo to find handcrafted ceramics, textiles, and other unique things.

Avoiding Exploitation: Make sure the things you buy are made under fair labor conditions. Avoid buying items that exploit workers or employ child labor. Fairtrade certificates can aid in identifying ethically made items.

Eco-Friendly Products: Choose souvenirs made of sustainable materials. Items manufactured from recycled or natural materials are not only environmentally sustainable but also frequently represent local culture and skill.

Cultural Sensitivity: Be aware of the cultural importance of goods. Some objects or cultural symbols may have sacred significance and should be acquired with care and knowledge. Avoid purchasing anything that may be deemed derogatory to the local culture.

Finally, traveling sustainably and responsibly in Guanajuato improves your experience while positively impacting the environment and the local people. By choosing eco-friendly activities, supporting local businesses, lowering your carbon footprint, and purchasing ethically, you can help Guanajuato remain a beautiful and thriving destination for years to come. Embracing these habits not only improves your travel experience but also builds a stronger connection with the places and people you visit.

Sample Itinerary

Planning a vacation to Guanajuato can be both thrilling and overwhelming owing to the abundance of sites and activities offered. To help you make the most of your stay, here's a complete sample schedule that spans five days and includes culture, history, and relaxation.

Day 1: Arrival
Morning: Arrival & Check-in
- Arrive in Guanajuato City and settle into your hotel. Choose a strategically situated hotel, such as Hotel Boutique 1850, for easy access to major attractions.

Afternoon: Explore the Historic Center
- Take a leisurely walk around the UNESCO World Heritage site.
- Visit the city's center, Jardín de la Unión, which is surrounded by cafés and restaurants.
- Explore the neighboring Teatro Juárez, an architectural marvel with breathtaking interiors.

Evening: Dinner and Night Walk

- Dine at Casa Valadez, a modern-day take on classic Mexican food.
- After supper, go for an evening stroll around the city's lovely lanes. Join a "callejoneada" trip, a traditional musical walking tour led by student musicians known as "Estudiantes," to see Guanajuato's distinct nightlife.

Day 2: Cultural & Historical Immersion

Morning: Museo de las Momias & Alhóndiga de Granaditas

- Visit the Museo de las Momias to see Guanajuato's famed mummies. The museum showcases naturally mummified remains discovered in the city.
- Visit the Alhóndiga de Granaditas, a historic granary turned museum that played an important part during Mexico's War of Independence. The structure itself is remarkable, and the displays offer detailed insights into the country's history.

Afternoon: University of Guanajuato & Lunch

- The university is noted for its remarkable architecture. Consider taking a guided tour to learn about the university's history and relevance.

- Have lunch at Truco 7, a small restaurant that serves authentic Mexican cuisine in a rustic environment.

Evening: Panoramic View and Dinner

- Take the funicular up to El Pípila monument for a panoramic view of the city as the sun sets.
- Enjoy dinner afterward. The monument honors a hero of the Mexican War of Independence and provides stunning vistas.
- Los Campos is noted for its inventive food and cozy environment, so have a relaxing supper there.

Day 3: Trip to San Miguel de Allende
Morning: Travel to San Miguel de Allende

- Depart early for San Miguel de Allende, which is around an hour and a half drive from Guanajuato.
- This charming town is famous for its well-preserved colonial architecture and thriving cultural scene.

Afternoon: Explore the Town
- Visit the Parroquia de San Miguel Arcángel, the iconic pink neo-Gothic church in the town's main square.
- Visit the local artisan markets and stores to get one-of-a-kind souvenirs and crafts.

Evening: Dinner & Return
- Visit Hecho en México, a well-known restaurant in San Miguel that serves both Mexican and foreign food.
- Return to Guanajuato City in the evening.

Day 4: Art, Museums, & Relaxation
Morning: Diego Rivera Museum & Cultural Exploration
- Begin your day visiting the Museo Casa Diego Rivera, the birthplace of the renowned Mexican muralist. The museum has a collection of his early works and personal belongings.
- Visit the Temple of San Diego and the nearby Jardin de la Reforma.

Afternoon: Museo Iconográfico del Quijote and Lunch

- Head to the Museo Iconográfico del Quijote, dedicated to Miguel de Cervantes' literary masterpiece. The museum features an extensive collection of art inspired by "Don Quixote."
- Enjoy a light lunch at Café Conquistador, known for its excellent coffee and pastries.

Evening: Relaxation and Dinner

- Relax at your hotel or explore nearby shops and cafés at your leisure.
- For supper, go to El Abue, a restaurant with a great menu of Mexican and foreign foods in a gorgeous setting.

Day 5: Outdoor Adventure & Departure
Morning: Hiking in the Sierra de Santa Rosa

- Take a morning hike in the Sierra de Santa Rosa mountains. Trails like "La Bufa" offer stunning views and a refreshing break from the city's hustle and bustle.

Afternoon: Relax & prepare for departure

- Return to Guanajuato City for a relaxing day. Visit previously overlooked locations or revisit beloved spots. Enjoy your farewell lunch at a neighborhood eatery. Panadería La Purísima is ideal for a leisurely lunchtime.

Evening: Departure

- Depending on your travel plans, prepare for your departure. Ensure you have transportation arranged to the airport or bus station.

This sample schedule combines cultural immersion, historical inquiry, and leisure to provide a thorough experience of Guanajuato. To make the most of your vacation, tailor the schedule to your interests and speed.

Conclusion

Guanajuato, with its colorful history, rich culture, and breathtaking scenery, provides an outstanding vacation experience to suit a wide range of interests. Guanajuato offers something for everyone, whether you're interested in colonial architecture, historical importance, or natural beauty.

The city's cobblestone streets and colorful buildings provide for a lovely environment that seems like going back in time. From the busy Mercado Hidalgo, where local merchants sell fresh fruit and homemade crafts, to the tranquil gardens of Sierra de Santa Rosa, every corner in Guanajuato tells a tale. Walking around the historic center, you'll come across architectural marvels such as the Teatro Juárez and the imposing University of Guanajuato, all of which highlight the city's rich legacy.

Guanajuato's cultural scene is equally captivating. The city is home to various museums, including the Museo de las Momias and the Museo Casa Diego Rivera, which provide insights into the region's history and cultural legacy. Festivals such as the International Cervantino Festival highlight the city's thriving cultural culture, attracting performers and viewers from all over the world. The colorful callejoneadas, or traditional musical walking tours, reflect the city's energetic culture and community-oriented lifestyle.

For those seeking outdoor experiences, the neighboring mountains and valleys provide great hiking, biking, and horseback riding options. The diversified environment provides spectacular vistas and opportunities to interact with nature. Sustainable and ethical tourism methods are progressively being used, ensuring that Guanajuato's natural and cultural assets are conserved for future generations.

Guanajuato's food is delightful, with a variety of classic and contemporary meals to enjoy. From street food escapades to gourmet dining experiences, the city's culinary choices will satisfy any taste. Supporting local restaurants and markets enhances your experience while also benefiting the neighborhood.

In essence, Guanajuato is a city that captures the heart and intellect. Its distinct combination of history, culture, and natural beauty results in a lively and intriguing destination. As you plan your trip, remember to appreciate the local customs, respect the environment, and thoroughly immerse yourself in Guanajuato's colorful culture. Guanajuato guarantees a fascinating and enriching experience, whether you're visiting for the first time or returning.

Made in the USA
Coppell, TX
19 December 2024

43170860R00056